Shimmer

Shimmer

Poems by

Robert Haight

© 2021 Robert Haight. All rights reserved.
This material may not be reproduced in any form, published,
reprinted, recorded, performed, broadcast,
rewritten or redistributed without
the explicit permission of Robert Haight.
All such actions are strictly prohibited by law.

Cover design by Shay Culligan

Cover photgraph by Steve Begnoche
American Coot Photography

ISBN: 978-1-954353-61-9

Kelsay Books
502 South 1040 East, A-119
American Fork, Utah, 84003

for Tomasa, always

Acknowledgments

Many thanks to the publications in which versions of the following poems have appeared:

Cortland Review: "Cornfield in Fog"

Encore: "Quicksand," "Spiders in June," "Shimmer"

Michigan Poetry Society Newsletter: "Crows"

Peninsula Poets: "Allergy Shot," "Removing a Hook"

Third Wednesday: "Enbridge Line Five," "Listening to John Coltrane's 'Crescent' While Looking Out at the Frozen Lake," "August Fishing," "Geometry," "Changing Season," "Elegy After the Dogs," "There May Come Back to You a Voice"

Contents

Cornfield in Fog	11
Quicksand	12
Allergy Shot	14
Removing a Hook	16
Spiders in June	18
Enbridge Line Five	19
Ephemera	20
Chuang Tzu Triolet	22
Shimmer	23
August Fishing	24
Changing Season	25
An Autumn	26
Brown Marmorated Stink Bugs	27
Elegy After the Dogs	28
May There Come Back to You a Voice	29
Crows	31
Geometry	32
Sinclair	34
A Spell of Warm Weather	35
Year End	36
Listening to John Coltrane's "Crescent" While Looking Out at the Frozen Lake	37
Three Lights in Early Winter	38

Cornfield in Fog

These monks
in their white robes
have fasted so long
only smiles
lean from their skeletons.

They are yellow teeth
and bones.

Tassel hats rattle
and silk sleeves swish
as they sweep the aisles
with brooms fashioned
from a stalk and leaves.

They whisper all morning
bow in the wind
then raise their heads
to the rising sun

the sky's
pristine blue dome.

Quicksand

Where did all the quicksand go?
When we were kids, it was everywhere,
swallowing horses, wagons, the men
wearing black hats who deserved it.
The sheriff would ride up
to the quicksand trap,
a bad guy up to his armpits
calling for help.
A rope and a horse
might drag him out.
But sometimes help arrived
too late and the camera
returned to hands
disappearing under muddy bubbles.
Even in the new suburbs
we knew it must be boiling after rains
where houses under construction
had dirt yards instead of lawns.
Watch out for the quicksand,
we'd yell before entering the open ribs
of the home through the wall studs.
There must have been quicksand
by the creek at the end
of the street before they culverted it
and laid a sidewalk over it
burying any trace.
Now the creek is gone, the woods
are gone and the houses
were long ago finished, sold
and re-sold. The suburbs are safe
and uniform as slices of Wonder Bread.

These days only fathers get sucked
under and disappear from time to time
in the unforeseen quicksand
of their corporate offices.

Allergy Shot

It's the way you take
the cotton ball
between your index finger
and thumb,
use it to search
the most fleshy
bulge of triceps,
swab the back
of my upper arm
then fan the skin
with your hand
before you remove
a syringe
from the rack of five
in their white plastic case,
pierce the rubber
stopper on the vial,
suck honey serum
into the cylinder
before the smooth
penetration into skin
where you have squeezed it
into a little mound,
the slow pressure
pushing the plunger down
as the fluid disappears,
my arm
filling with it,
my arm
joined by the hollow needle
to your hand,

your arm, your body
standing next to mine,
this intimacy, this pinprick
of pain and concern.

Removing a Hook

The ones that pierce the flesh
of a finger or meat of the hand
only up to the barb
can be pulled easily
like a loose tooth

but if the hook goes deep
buried below the barb
you'll need forceps
maybe a sharp knife or scalpel
and some alcohol to clean
the skin and settle the nerves.

Twist up and see what comes.
If muscle rises with the steel
don't give up hope.
A few know a trick
they do with fishing line,
wrapping it around the shank
just above the skin
and with a jerk snap the hook free.

Others use pliers to cut if off,
then push the shank back
through the hole it made.
At emergency rooms, doctors
cut a smooth line
to open a track around the hook
so it will pull like a weed.

And if you give up trying
you can always wear it as a statement
of rebellion with the same pride
some show in their piercings,
hooks dangling from ear lobes,
septums, tongues, navels,
the clinking jewelry of bad casters.

Spiders in June

All through the night
they worked

at their weaving
spinning gossamer

from leaf to stalk,
stalk to weed,

from spindly branch
to flower petal,

looming their fabric
under silver moonlight,

stitching the beach
and the roadsides

with their summer
cloth until

when the sun appeared
the morning webbed

their filaments,
every ray of light

sticking to the threads
of their invisible presence.

Enbridge Line Five

What happens when all the light
spills from the full moon
onto the lake, a slick of silver

spreading to the edges of darkness?
I wade out into the night
with cords and pink balloons

to rope it in before moonlight
drifts all the way through the Straits,
chokes Mackinac and Bois Blanc

oozes south through Lake Huron
to St. Clair, and down the sunset coast
toward Gary, the clanging sailboats

and mumbling cruisers strangled with it
the beach sand drifted with its snow,
the old folks telling their grandchildren

it was once as blue as the sky
and people took off their clothes
and dove right into it.

Ephemera

I wallowed for years
in that warm, dark room
with the shades drawn,
its thick silt blanket
pressing my legs
wrapped around my carapace
in the quiet below
the earth's perils.

I live in muck the way
you thrive in air
or perhaps more your dive
to the bottom of a lake,
sounds muffling until they disappear,
a murky night swallowing stars.

Then this calling
I didn't so much choose
as was chosen by

crawling into the light,
the dizzying leaves,
the breeze hardening my shell.
Sometimes you must clutch
the jagged bark of a trunk
and hold on

until you explode
out of yourself,
the grass and swaying trees,
the glittering river below

as you thrum the clear panes
of your new wings
and for one golden evening
play the music of summer.

Chuang Tzu Triolet

The sound of water says what I think
surge after surge across the lake
foam over boulders, rise and sink
the voice of water says not to think.
My dogs wade in and lap a drink
slapped by waves each sip they take.
The sound of water is what I think
nowhere to go, no plans to make.

Shimmer

Waves of water
rippling above the water
the light glinting
off the lake

on the highways too
rising from black asphalt
as if the road simmered
on a summer afternoon.

They say it's all mirage,
you know, though closer you
never arrive, the prism
splitting into its rainbow

the moon balanced
inside a drop of dew.
Cool blue lights the dark grass
tiny lanterns in the night.

I've swum out into the lake
toward the light
that danced on the rim
of where water meets sky

there was nothing there
to hold onto but I could feel
the warmth of the light
on my skin.

August Fishing

Late summer
gets shaggy
with wildflowers

trout idle in the shade
and remember evenings
of mayflies

until a grasshopper
blown into the river
by a sudden gust

thrashes its legs
and needs to be saved
from drowning

by the brown trout
who picks up
the grasshopper

in its mouth
and spits it out
on the mossy top

of a fallen log
and just that fast
is gone.

Changing Season

It had been less humid and cooler
for a few days, a breeze

from the north though only late July
when I heard over

our roof through the open windows
the honk of a Canada goose

stroking south from one lake
to another, and it left

the thought that this sound
could signal the beginning

of autumn though so many
times meaning has been only

my creation: that woman dangling
her red high heel

and smiling in the restaurant
someone waving in the grocery store

to their friend standing just
behind me.

An Autumn

Stacking wood in the mid-October sunshine
a summer-warm day, light breeze rattling
the changing leaves, a winter's worth
of warmth clunking into rows
as my son and I carry logs from the heap
in the grass to the neatly arranged stacks
at the back of the yard and while we work
wiping away dust and sweat from our faces
the squirrels race around burying acorns,
some squadrons of geese honk by
in their formations to descend
down the runways at the end of the lake,
weeds gone to seed waving in the field
behind us as the wind swishes its
skirts and the day radiates light and rainbows.

Brown Marmorated Stink Bugs

When they arrived a few years ago
through invisible cracks in our house
on the warmest late September afternoons
to crawl along the walls and ceiling

seeking a good spot to spend
the winter, we had never seen anything
like these lima beans on legs

that carried the odor of cilantro
within them and squirted that scented
juice over any hand that pressed
them too tightly. They supposedly

had been living in the corn
and soybean fields all summer,
had traveled to us from some states

in the south or east though they never
seemed to fly over a few feet
and waddled like old men and women.
They packed into cardboard boxes

in the garage, gathered like dead
leaves in the corners of window sills
until the Michigan winter arrived.

When they froze they left a strong
whiff of summer greenery,
the one gift they could offer us
for staying at our home.

Elegy After the Dogs

Now Mag and Rose have returned
home as ashes in plastic bags
topped with a twist tie

within cardboard boxes with a card
attached to each stating the date
of their transformation

from fur and blood and ways of being
to something that is them
and not them at the same time.

The air has never been this still
without their wagging tails
fanning it. They no longer

have any interest in scooping
up pieces of food I drop on the floor.
Yet something of them remains,

calls me over to touch the boxes
before I head off to bed
for the night

to say to each,
Goodnight sweet girl as if they
can hear me.

May There Come Back to You a Voice

a line from Galway Kinnell

I was always looking forward
to that time when things
would be easier, when
the appointment would be
over, when the deal would be
done, when the rapids would be
crossed and I could begin
my life again heading west
into the sun from the bank
on the other side.
But I've hiked through that place
where the woods were thick,
where the light fell apart,
where the mosquitos droned
an electrical whine all day,
where the swamp continued
on and on, the boot sucking muck
swallowing my legs and I could see
then how that guy just lost it
and laid down and died
in the shade under a pine,
I could see how that young couple
wandered in circles while the county
road was only a few hundred yards away
and I tell myself to do one thing
and then the next and to stay
out of the woods and instead wade
in the river and even where
it's deep and piled with log jams
and boulders, to hug the bank
but continue in the water anyway

because it will end up somewhere
where the canoes come out
or go in, where the bridge crosses,
where the beach is sandy, sunny
and shallow opening into the lake
and you can see kites in the air
in the blue distance.

Crows

Every morning a man walked out to the woods to listen. Soon he believed could translate the language of crows. He took notes on their conversations as they gathered and scattered in the leafy tops of trees. He recorded the crows to later study them as they pecked at roadkill in the ditches along the sides of the lonely county roads as the heaped winter snow melted into the grass of spring. He tried to speak back to the crows, certain they remembered him by the wary gleam in their yellow eyes, but they never acknowledged they understood his caws. He began to love them whether he understood them or not, whether they understood him or not, and so every day he returned to them and watched them and listened. After he had grown very old, one day the man died and was taken to his grave in the township cemetery followed by a flock of very raucous crows.

Geometry

My little woodstove
takes a sixteen inch log
so the manual says
and the guy who cuts
my wood knows that
and tries to saw them
about that length
though occasionally
he will cut them too long
which I discover
when adding a log
to a roaring blaze
a knob or two at the end
sticking out through the door
which I can no longer close
the far end already ignited
and flaming as I try to move
the piece into a more
diagonal angle
and then raise one end
to see if that might buy
a few inches or turn
the whole thing
in the other direction
as if magically the stove
will stretch to accommodate it.
And sometimes, magically, it does
and I close and latch the door.
But other times I accept
that it will never fit
and walk through the house
with my flaring taper in hand

setting off the fire alarms
as I head to the garage
and through it to the back yard
my Roman candle sputtering sparks,
the neighbors looking
through their window
thinking I must again
have something to celebrate.

Sinclair

Just passed the heart of Cassopolis
where the bank in its new building
gleams in the metallic sunlight,
where most of the other storefronts
empty onto an empty curb,
some of them still sporting signs
of the prosperity that once lived here,
Rexall Drugs, the Wards appliance store, the card shop
all vacant glass and dusty tiled floors,
the Wounded Minnow bar still open,
hanging on to that need for a sweating beer,
and down the hill and around the curve
of the lake, a Sinclair gas station
that no longer sells gas, no pumps
in front of the building, but freshly painted
bright white, the garage door looking
as though you could still pull in to get
your oil changed by some guys dressed
in blue cotton work clothes with red rags
hanging from a pocket and out front
the tall sign at the top of its mast
with a green dinosaur on it, a brontosaurus,
looking ahead with its long neck outstretched
to where the road disappears into miles of corn.

A Spell of Warm Weather

For those looking forward
it was early April, a breeze
carrying sunlight rubbing
its fingers through the fur
of the grass and for those
looking back it was late
September, a wood fire
in the evening, smoke curling
upward to the stars.
It was easy to forget Halloween
iced in and frozen, the skeletons
wrapping their arms
around their ribs and tap
dancing from a low limb.
And though everyone knows
February is the shortest month
in days the tires spin so slowly
that time stops along the road
in the dark and wonders if it's lost.
We've had these warm
December days before,
no white Christmas, New Years
the golf course waving its flags.
We come out of doors
with looks of wonder
on our faces
the sheep we counted
disappearing up the hill
into the distance.

Year End

I'm finally going through the paper
address cards stored in a wooden box
on the kitchen counter, a throwback

to the years before phone and computer
electronic address books, tossing
into the fire the cards with the names

and addresses of those who died
this year or last or the years before that,
tossing the cards of some old neighbors

who moved away and disappeared, tossing
the cards of businesses that painted
or did plumbing or electrical years ago

and that have since gone out of business
or retired to Florida, throwing out the wood
guy who came one year but never again

the card of my mother's next door
neighbor in Detroit before she was moved
to the nursing home in Chicago

before she died a decade ago, tossing away
these cards that have no use beyond memory
which in itself offers no reason to keep anything

the cards becoming before quickly
turning to ash a momentary flame
a small burst of brightness.

Listening to John Coltrane's "Crescent" While Looking Out at the Frozen Lake

Recorded live in Tokyo
almost fifty years ago
but through the mystery of radio waves

I am listening to it now,
Coltrane long dead and disappeared,
his band disbanded and off to the rest

of the music of their lives.
His wife Alice plays piano. Pharoah Sanders
sounds the low foghorn of bass clarinet

and Jimmy Garrison plucks the standup bass.
Someone whistles from the crowd during a pause
in the solo, the moment captured as if all

those years since, the graying hair, the losses
and the joys, were just daydreams
to be reborn in the darkness

of five o'clock am filling the kitchen here
thanks to the reach of public radio
that has arched across the Straits

into the pines and cedars, snow covered now,
the lake nothing more than white desolation,
the crowds of last summer gone

of next summer not yet born
and Coltrane's saxophone fluttering
like a gull on the beach

that instead of leaving
when the season changed
decided to stay through it all.

Three Lights in Early Winter

Four a.m. darkness. Snow
settled in to itself.

Piles of moonlight
lantern the way
to the wood pile.

Songbirds have fled
the cold and the crows
that remain deepen
the shadows of pine
branches. In silence
the owl too
waits for small tracks
in the snow.

Soon dawn will bring
the visible world
when animals
disappear in the light.
The breeze will lose
its mystery.
Now just fire flames,
here and there
a yard light
casting a blue pond
on a patch of grass.

About the Author

Robert Haight has published two full-length poetry collections, *Emergences and Spinner Falls* (New Issues Poetry and Prose) and *Feeding Wild Birds* (Mayapple Press), a chapbook, *Water Music* (Ridgeway Press), and has written essays and articles on fly fishing, the environment, education and spirituality for a variety of anthologies, journals and magazines. He divides his time between the Lower and Upper Peninsula of Michigan.

www.ingramcontent.com/pod-product-compliance
Lightning Source LLC
Chambersburg PA
CBHW021029090426

42738CB00007B/947